KAREN IN WONDERLAND

by **L.K. PETERSON**

illustrated by **DEBORAH BERK**

Front cover by Deborah Berk

For more on Now What Media Books,
please visit nowwhatmedia.com/nowwhatbooks.html

Furiouser and furiouser!
— Karen

DEDICATION / DISCLAIMER

Any resemblance of the title character to anyone I've ever known named Karen is unintentional, coincidental and more-or-less impossible, as none of them are anything at all like this.

L.K. PETERSON

L.K. Peterson is a writer whose books include *Fairly Grim Tales*, *The Da Vinci Cold*, *Further Adventures*, *Talk to the Hair* and *Political Animals: Now What Anthology #2* and is responsible for the website *Ant Farmer's Almanac*. He lives in Brooklyn, NY with his wife, an illustrator.

DEBORAH BERK

Deborah Berk is an illustrator, sculptor, photographer and former art therapist. She lives in Brooklyn, NY with two emotional-support turtles and her husband, who is a writer.

TABLE OF CONTENTS

1: UNEXPECTED GUESTS

Karen was relaxing in her yard one hot summer day, sipping Long Island ice tea and popping CBD gummies when she saw a rabbit — and not a white one — run by, talking to itself excitedly, a messenger bag slung over its shoulder.

This made Karen angrier than she'd been about anything since before breakfast, and Karen could be angrier about more things before breakfast than most people can be in a week. "That's not right!" she said to herself, "The Homeowners Association has strict rules for pets and rabbits are not allowed. Whoever owns that rabbit is looking at a serious fine!"

Karen grabbed her pistol and her cell phone and went after the rabbit. One way or another, she was determined to take a shot.

She chased after it, shouting, "Get off my lawn! You don't belong here!" and "I'm calling the cops!"

The rabbit headed for a far corner of the yard and jumped into a large hole Karen hadn't noticed before.

She leapt in after it.

As she tumbled down the hole, Karen realized she was floating not falling and thought, "That idiot gardener is so fired. He's managed to leave a deep hole in my yard and screw up gravity!"

Landing at the bottom with a mild bump, Karen didn't see the rabbit but along the floorboards just across from her was a small wooden door, closed over a cartoon style mouse hole. Next to it was a side table on which sat a bottle labeled, "Don't Drink Me!"

"No bottle is going to tell me what to do!" harrumphed Karen. She took a swig but it tasted terrible and she spit most of it out. "I'm not paying for this swill!" she said to no one in particular.

Still, she'd swallowed enough of whatever it was to have some effect. She suddenly felt herself getting larger and larger until she took up the whole room!

"This can't be happening to me! It isn't fair!" she exclaimed, "I have a Peleton!"

Karen felt very sorry for herself. Her eyes got watery and soon she was gushing tears that quickly flooded the room and, as they did, shrank Karen back to her previous size. Then even smaller, so that now she was swimming in a deep pool of her own giant-self's tears.

As she treaded water, a little brown mouse swam past her.

"Hey," she yelled at the mouse, "Where do you think you're going?"

The mouse squeaked something Karen didn't understand which could only mean it was a foreigner trying to illegally sneak onto her property.

"Go back to where you came from," shouted Karen, "And while you're in my country, speak English!"

The mouse dove under the surface
and pushed open the door. Like a sink
draining after its plug is pulled, water
gushed through the doorway, taking the
mouse, and then tiny Karen, with it.

2. NOT UNDER MY BACKYARD!

Karen was only submerged for a moment or two before she lifted her head above the water to see she was now in a stream. It wasn't very wide or deep and she was easily able to swim over to and crawl onto the shoreline.

She shook herself as dry as she could and snarled, "Well, this is gonna be a bad hair day!"

She glanced up to see a very odd couple of fellows staring down at her. They looked alike, were dressed identically and standing so close together they might have been attached.

"What the hell?" demanded Karen.

"We are Tweedledumb," answered the one on the left, "And Twiddledidee," said the one on the right, adding, "We've been trying to reach you about your car's extended warranty."

"And the IRS wants to review your case; press "1" to speak to an agent or you may face persecution," said Tweedledumb.

"Did you know," said Twiddledidee, "This one simple trick can cure back pain, computer viruses and reduce your utility bills?"

It was at this moment, when she could have really used one or both of them, Karen realized she'd lost her phone and her gun somewhere between the fall and the flood.

"Is your personal information secure enough?" asked Tweedledumb, "Tell us your mother's first pet's favorite color so we can evaluate how to better protect your privacy!"

Every time they spoke, Karen got furiouser and furiouser.

"Hot singles in your area want to meet you," said Twidledidee, with a wink and a sly grin.

"Who's in charge here! I demand to see the manager!" shrieked Karen.

"All operators are busy with other customers right now. Your waiting time is approximately 42 minutes," said the pair simultaneously.

"You may have won a Caribbean cruise!" yipped Tweedledumb.

"I don't have to listen to this!" fumed Karen as she brushed past the pair and toward some trees, "I'm getting out of here."

"Would you take a brief survey and leave some feedback?" hollered Twiddledidee after her, sounding a little desperate.

Without looking back, Karen said, "Here's your feedback, assholes," gave them the finger and kept walking.

3. DEEP DODO

A path through the trees led to a clearing. In it, Karen saw a strange bird standing alone.

It was a Dodo.

"A Dodo bird!" she said, "That can't be. You're extinct!"

"Really?" replied the Dodo, turning to look at Karen, "I felt fine when I got up this morning."

"Yes, really. And, extinct or not, you shouldn't be able to talk!"

"So, I don't exist and I can't talk, eh?" said the Dodo, "But here I am talking to you and there you are talking to me."

"That's right!" blustered Karen, "I know an extinct bird when I see one and if I say you don't exist, you don't!"

Of course, what really had Karen so unnerved wasn't that she was talking to an extinct bird that shouldn't talk, it was if anyone found out an extinct talking bird lived under it, her yard could be declared some kind of protected extinct talking bird wildlife habitat and she'd need a mountain of permits from tree-huggers just to get the lawn mowed.

Without saying another word, the Dodo reached over and bit Karen on the ankle.

"Ow! Son of a bitch!" yelped Karen, "That hurt!"

"Maybe so but, since I don't exist," said the Dodo, "It'll only leave a fake bruise."

"You just wait until I find the manager," Karen fumed, "You're gonna be in so much trou. . ."

Before she could finish, Karen saw that the Dodo was facing her, head down, pawing the ground one foot at a time and flexing its stubby, useless little wings.

It was going to charge at her.

Before it could, Karen took off running.

4. THE TOKING CATERPILLAR

Karen ran as far as she could which really wasn't all that far. But it was far enough that when she looked back there was no sign of the Dodo.

She stopped to catch her breath and noticed a very large caterpillar. Really large. Taller than her by a foot or more. Taller than you, probably. It was sitting atop the biggest shiitake mushroom you ever saw and smoking from an enormous bong.

Karen walked around the mushroom to face the caterpillar who didn't move but shifted his gaze just enough to be looking directly at her and said nothing.

The caterpillar didn't blink so neither did she.

This went on for a while.

Just as Karen wondered if caterpillars even can blink and whether she'd got herself into a staring contest she couldn't win, the caterpillar exhaled a cloud of pungent smoke.

"Who . . ." it said in a wispy belch, "Are you?"

"I might ask you the same thing!" replied Karen.

"I suppose you might but, I already know who I am and I asked you first."

"My name is Karen and you're in – under – my backyard and I want to know what you think you're doing here!"

"Well now, do you want to know what I think I'm doing here or what I am doing here?" replied the caterpillar, "You can see for yourself what I'm doing although, admittedly, it may not be what I think I'm doing."

"Can't I get a straight answer from anyone down here? You're as bad as that Dodo!"

"Oh, so you've seen Dodo?" said the caterpillar, "I thought he was still extinct."

"That's what I told him," replied Karen.

"Oh, he gets very upset when you tell him that," said the caterpillar, gravely, "I don't blame him, really, poor fellow. Imagine everyone saying you don't exist anymore, right to your face."

"But Dodos are extinct!" said Karen, getting more aggravated than usual, which is saying something.

"Exactly!" said the caterpillar in a very satisfied tone, as if Karen had proved his point. He relit the bong and took a huge hit.

"Look," said, Karen, "Is there anyone around here who knows who's in charge?"

The caterpillar coughed out smoke right into Karen's face.

"Ooh, gross," she whined, "You shouldn't blow smoke at people!" while making a big show of waving it away.

"Snowflake," said the caterpillar as he pointed behind where Karen was standing, "Maybe that way."

As she turned to walk away, Karen muttered loudly enough to be heard "Call me when you've turned into a butterfly, loser."

But the caterpillar had taken another big hit off his bong and paid her no mind.

5. THE WORCESTERSHIRE CAT

As she walked along the path through the woods grumbling to herself, Karen heard a voice.

"Are you looking for me?"

Karen stopped and looked around but didn't see anyone.

"Up here," the voice said.

Looking up, she saw a very well-fed tabby cat lounging lazily on a tree branch, grinning from ear to ear.

"Are you the manager?" asked Karen.

"I manage well enough, I suppose, if that's what you mean," answered the cat.

"No, that's not what I mean. I mean are you the one in charge around here?"

"There's someone in charge?" asked the cat, perking up, and seeming more interested, "I wonder who that might be?"

"Well, whoever it is, I demand to see them!" shouted Karen.

"Be careful what you wish for," cautioned the cat. "You might check with the Mad Hatter and his Tea Partiers. They have lots of theories about who's behind what. One of them might even be right," adding after a moment's thought, "Why would you want to know something like that, anyway?"

"You're under my yard without my permission and I want all of you to leave at once!"

"Oh," said the cat languidly, "I'm leaving," adding with a chuckle, "Just not all of me at once."

With that, the cat's toothy grin got even toothier, then, starting from his tail, he evaporated into thin air until the only part of him Karen could still see was his smile which lingered for a moment after the rest of him had disappeared and then, just like that, it too was gone.

"See you around fur ball," said Karen to the branch where the cat had been.

"No you won't," replied the cat's voice from seemingly nowhere.

6. IT'S A MAD, MAD, MAD, MAD TEA PARTY

Karen continued along the path until she came to an unkempt meadow with weeds and dandelions coming up to her knees.

At the far end of this meadow she could see a picnic table with two or three figures seated around it and many empty chairs.

She waded toward them through the wildflowers and, as she got closer, could make out the trio. At the head of the table sat a smallish man wearing an Uncle Sam-style top hat so many sizes too big for him that it pushed his ears out straight out sideways, covered his

eyes and rested on the tip of his nose. To his left was a March Hare, wearing a red fez, its tassel wrapped around and dangling from his left ear and, in a teacup on the table in front of them, a dormouse wearing a bishop's miter.

They were all pretending to sip tea.

Karen stepped up to the table and plopped down into one of the empty chairs facing the trio. Settling into her seat, Karen sensed that the Hare and the dormouse both seemed very, very angry.

She felt right at home.

The Hatter continued doing what he'd been doing all along which, Karen could see now, was folding tricorn hats out of tinfoil and stacking them onto a chair beside him.

The dormouse and the March Hare meanwhile, glared at Karen with open hostility.

"What?" Karen asked brusquely. "You, dormouse, what's your problem?"

"Please!" replied the dormouse haughtily, "I may have been born a dormouse but I identify as a church mouse and expect to be treated accordingly," he said adjusting his miter for emphasis, "You may address me as Monsignor, Your Bishopness, the Very Reverend Churchmouse-Formerly-Known-as-Dormouse and, after office hours, you can call me Ray.

"What if you were to become a Cardinal?" asked the March Hare.

"Don't be silly," sniffed the dormouse, "Why would I want to be a bird? Besides," he went on, "You're a fine one to talk. You call yourself a March Hare but you're still a hare no matter what month it is."

"It's an old family name," said the Hare in a huff, "Measuring and naming units of time is an entirely human construct and I refuse to be bound by it."

"Still," said the Hatter, "It is a handy way to know when you are at."

"Nonsense," said the Hare, dismissively, "It is always today, no matter what you call it. Tomorrow doesn't exist because as soon as it does it's today, and yesterday, being a memory, is whatever you say it was."

The dormouse seemed about to speak but, before he could, the Hatter turned to Karen and said, "You're arrogant and over-entitled and, while we like that in a complete stranger, if you're going to join us, you'll have to choose a hat," as he gestured to a pile of them in the middle of the table.

They were mostly ball caps for sports teams from before their names and mascots were deemed too offensive and had to be changed, along with a handful emblazoned with political slogans that hadn't aged well and, at the center, a Viking helmet, complete with horns.

"I'm not here to join you," said Karen, firmly, "I'm here for answers."

"Oh, dear," replied the Hatter, "All we have are questions."

"But we do have lots and lots of them," said the dormouse cheerfully, "Good ones!"

"Yes," added the March Hare, "Maybe your answer is in the form of a question?"

"I demand to see the manager!" shouted Karen, startling the trio.

After a stunned pause, the Hatter, the March Hare and the dormouse regained their composure and began applauding daintily.

"Well done!" exclaimed the Hatter, "A declarative sentence!"

"What a delightful twist," said the dormouse, "I really didn't see that coming."

"Sounded almost like the Red Queen herself there for a moment," said the March Hare.

"Wait, what? The Red Queen?" asked Karen, "She sounds like somebody who'd be in charge."

"She certainly thinks she is," said the March Hare.

"Well, her guards with the spears," noted the dormouse, "Can be fairly persuasive."

"Yes, she's definitely in charge at the palace," agreed the Hatter, "But, outside of it," he shrugged, "Only if you think so."

"Oh," said the dormouse, looking behind where Karen was seated, "There's the

Red Queen's stupid rabbit messenger
now. Late as usual."

"You're late again!" the Hatter, the March
Hare and the dormouse taunted in
unison.

Karen turned around and, sure enough,
bent over and trying to catch its breath,
was the very same not-white rabbit with
the messenger bag she'd chased down
here.

"I know, I know," he replied wearily,
turning to look over at them, "Oh,
whatever am I going to. . ."

When the rabbit and Karen's eyes met,
the rabbit froze in terror.

"You!" shrieked Karen.

"Aiieee!" shrieked the rabbit.

The rabbit scrambled to pick up his messenger bag and get it over his shoulder but Karen sprang out of her seat and grabbed him by the ears, lifting him off the ground before he could run away.

"Ooh, that's gotta hurt," said the March Hare, wincing at the sight.

"Please, let me go!" cried the rabbit, "She's gonna be so mad!"

"I'm here now and I'm already plenty mad!" growled Karen.

"I advise you to not answer any questions without your attorney present," said the Hatter.

"I don't have an attorney!" cried the rabbit at the same moment Karen barked, "I haven't asked him any questions!"

"Well," said the Hatter, "It's settled then," and he turned back to his folding.

"Take me to your Red Queen!" Karen snarled at the rabbit.

"Okay, I mean, I was going there anyway," adding, "Do you have to carry me by my ears? It's very uncomfortable."

Karen leaned toward the Hatter and snatched the top hat off his head, turned it upside down and shoved the rabbit into it. She glanced at the hats piled on the table, grabbed and put on the Viking helmet. It fit well and felt good.

The Hatter, meanwhile, reached under the table and pulled out another top hat just as big as the previous one and put it on.

`Karen looked down at the rabbit, "Okay, bunny boy, we're off to see the queen," she said firmly, "Which way?"

The rabbit pointed toward a narrow path through the weeds and Karen started walking.

As she moved out of sight, the Hatter said, "I wonder what she's so mad about?"

"We'll never know," replied the March Hare.

"I wonder if she does?" mused the dormouse.

7. RED QUEEN FOR A DAY

"Are you sure this is the right way?" Karen asked suspiciously, after walking for a while.

"It's the only way," replied the rabbit from the bottom of the top hat.

Karen had noticed the landscape around them seemed tidier and the path smoother, gradually changing from a dusty dirt trail to a smoothly paved walkway.

"Why do you want to see the Red Queen, anyway?" asked the rabbit, his nose peeking over the top of the hat's upturned brim but keeping his ears tucked down and out of reach, "Most people try to avoid her."

"I wish to register a complaint,"
answered Karen flatly.

"Oh!" replied the rabbit, "Nobody's ever
done that before." After a moment's
thought he asked, "What makes you
think she'll care? I mean, things are the
way they are because she's in charge,
and that's just the way she likes them.
Why would she change anything?"

"Because I say so."

The rabbit groaned and sank deeper into
the hat.

Up ahead was a neatly clipped two
story-tall hedge with the conical towers
and crenellated roofline of a fairy tale
style castle rising from behind it. At an
arched entry through the greenery a
pair of guards stood at attention, their

uniforms were decorated like playing cards, the Four and Five of Hearts, specifically.

As Karen approached the archway, she asked the rabbit, "Okay, we're here. Now what?"

The rabbit popped his head up from the hat and nodded at the guards who, recognizing him, snapped to attention and stepped aside to let them through.

Karen would never admit it but she was more than a little impressed.

"What, no moat?" she asked sarcastically as they went through the long leafy corridor.

"Not necessary," replied the Rabbit sincerely, ignoring Karen's snark, "The palace is surrounded by an extra-thick hedge maze. Even those who know it can get lost in there for days. Some who've gone in are never seen again."

Given the length of the passageway, Karen could almost believe it.

They finally emerged into a large courtyard. Karen noticed right away that the palace was much grander and fancier than her house or any other house in her neighborhood. This really pissed her off.

At the far end of the grounds a small crowd of guards and courtiers was gathered around a mini-golf course.

Everyone was focused on what could only be the Red Queen. Short and squat, with a large head made all the more

prominent by an upswept heart-shaped hairdo, she was dressed in regal finery; velvet brocade dress with an impressive bustle and, hanging around her neck, a clutch of pearls. But it was the bejeweled crown topping off the whole ensemble that was the dead giveaway.

The Red Queen pulled a pink flamingo from the bunch of them jammed into a golf bag held by her caddy (the Nine of Hearts) and took a couple of test swings.

At one side of the course was the royal throne, unoccupied at the moment but with a "RESERVED FOR ROYAL PERSONAGES" place card on the seat, and across the lawn from that, a table at which Tweedledumb and Twiddledidee sat as closely together as they has been standing when Karen first saw them.

The pair was speaking softly into a single microphone set in front of them, taking turns narrating the action in the hushed manner of pro golf announcers.

"Her nibs is lining up for her last shot of the day..."

"Yes, the windmill is always a tricky one, what with both the mill and the wind to consider."

"What number club has she pulled out? I can't quite tell from here."

"It's a flamingo. They're not numbered."

"You've really gotta hand it to that bird, getting swung around like that. It must be awfully dizzy and sore this far into the game."

"Oh, yes. I believe this is the same one she used at the clown's mouth, the lighthouse and the pirate ship."

"She's putting pretty well today, I think she may be on track to set a new course record..."

"She always does!"

"Yes and, wait, what's this? Someone is heading toward the course. A woman with frizzy hair, wearing a Viking helmet and carrying an oversize top hat upside down, like it's a bucket or something . . . She's heading straight for the Red Queen. I've never seen anything like this, such a brazen breach of protocol."

"She's right up to her highness now who's noticed her and turned to face her. Maybe if we stop talking and lean in, we can hear them. . ."

"What's the meaning of this!" demanded the Red Queen.

"I'm here to register a complaint!"

"A what!?!" sputtered the Red Queen.

Karen reached into the hat and pulled up the not-white rabbit by his ears.

The Red Queen gasped in astonishment, then smiled with delight and began clapping enthusiastically.

"Ah, pulling a rabbit out of a hat! Such a classic magic trick! I love it! Now," she said, pushing her caddy toward Karen, "Saw him in half!"

"No. This is my complaint," barked Karen, shoving the rabbit closer to the queen's face.

The Red Queen pulled a pair of pince nez glasses from her cleavage, clipped them to her nose and squinted at the rabbit.

"Oh, Oswald! There you are!"

"Sorry I'm late, your majesty," stammered the rabbit, sheepishly, "This is, eh, Karen, uh, so, eh, funny story. . ."

"Nonsense," said the queen, "You're always late so, you're right on time."

"Ahem!" Karen snorted.

"Oh, yes," said the Red Queen turning to face Karen and seeming quite imperiously perturbed, "You have some complaint about my royal messenger?"

"Him. You. And everyone else down here," replied Karen, "You're under my property without my say-so, see. I'll have you know that I'm on the HOA's committee of Audits and Control, and you're in violation of no fewer than 37 of our rules, regulations and statutes, starting with a hedge that is way over the maximum height, un-permitted non-standard ostentatious structural design and decor, the owning and operating of rabbits, trespassing. . ."

Karen paused briefly to take a breath as the growing fear in the Red Queen's eyes spurred her on.

"Oh, and municipal ordinances! Unauthorized tunnels and water features! Harboring extinct animals! Public use of illicit substances! Unlicensed hat manufacturing and who knows how many un-filed and unpaid city, county and state fees, taxes, surcharges . . . you'd better hope you have a good lawyer and a good accountant . . ."

As she spoke, Karen got more worked up, moving toward the Red Queen who took a step back for every step Karen took forward.

". . . And you've got this guy tearing up my backyard and doing . . ." Karen stopped mid-sentence, realizing she really didn't know what the not-white rabbit had been up to. She reached into the hat and yanked out the messenger bag.

She opened it and rifled through its contents as the Red Queen looked on nervously.

"So, what've we got here," Karen said as she pulled out various items, "Take-out menus, Bed Bath & Beyond coupons and. . ." she paused as she realized the enormity of what she was looking at, "My list of the neighbors' Wifi passwords!"

The Red Queen, already visibly terrified, looked anxiously to the guards on either side of her.

"Get me out of here!" she cried. The guards (the Seven and Ten of Hearts) lifted her by the armpits and jumped through the hedge and disappeared into the maze, knocking her crown off as they went.

"Oh, sure, yeah, that's it, run away!" Karen shouted after them, "Don't think I won't find you!"

She looked down at the crown, picked it up, took off the Viking helmet and set the crown atop her head in its place.

The crowd, including guards who hadn't been close enough to the queen to escape with her, stood still in shocked silence.

Karen glared at the courtiers and, as she scanned the group, they dropped to one knee, bowed their heads and said more-or-less in unison, "All hail, Queen Karen!"

"That's more like it," she growled back at them, just to make it clear they weren't in for some sort of benevolent monarchy.

She grabbed the exhausted flamingo her predecessor had dropped, strode over to the throne and bellowed, "There are going to be some changes made around here," then noticed from the corner of her eye, on a high tree branch over her shoulder, the emerging outlines of the Worcestershire cat, his bright smile already visible.

Pausing for dramatic effect, Karen swatted away the "RESERVED" place card and swung herself onto the throne but, the minute her butt hit the seat cushion the whole thing collapsed beneath her and she crashed to the ground, jolting herself pretty good and knocking the crown off.

Karen sat up quickly, shook her head and looked around only to see that she was back in her own yard, tangled up in a broken lawn chair and holding her cell phone instead of a flamingo.

In a tree just above her, she thought she saw the cat's grin, fading into the foliage.

Other Now What Books
Find out more at www.nowwhatmedia.com

Political Animals: Now What Anthology No. 2

Used / Reused

Taking Liberties

Silver Linings Plague Book

George Washington Back in New York City

Gertrude et Alice

Trump Tweets Alt-American History

Talk to the Hair

Flick and Flak: More Poison Capsule Reviews

The Golem's Voice

Further Adventures: Now What Anthology No. 1

PK in the Terrarium

Downtown Drowned

The Da Vinci Cold

Go the F✳✳k Back to Work!

Fairly Grim Tales

Love the Sinner, Hate the Cinema

Inx Battle Lines

Gertrude's Follies